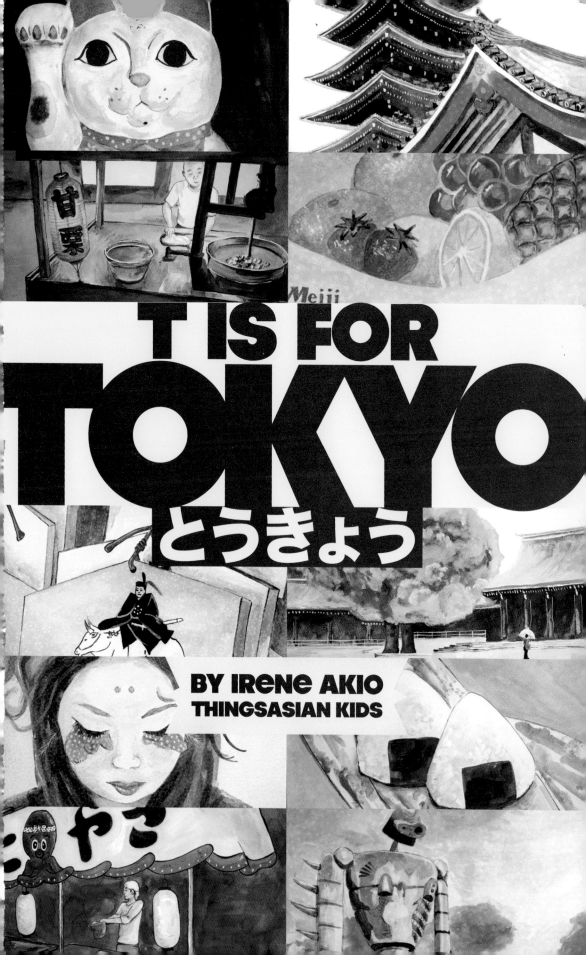

T IS FOR
TOKYO
とうきょう

BY IReNe AKIO
THINGSASIAN KIDS

"To my parents, Penny Corbett and Terumasa Akio,
who gave me the gift of two cultures." - I.A.

T is for Tokyo
By Irene Akio
Copyright ©2010 ThingsAsian Press

Edited by Janet Brown
Japanese translation by Atsuko Kobayashi
Cover and book design by Janet McKelpin

For information regarding permissions, write to:
ThingsAsian Press
3230 Scott Street
San Francisco, California 94123 USA
info@thingsasianpress.com
www.thingsasianpress.com
thingsasiankids.thingsasian.com
Printed in Singapore by Tien Wah Press

ISBN 13: 978-1-934159-23-1
ISBN 10: 1-934159-23-9

"Papa, tell me again about the city I was born in."

「 ねえ パパ わたしはどんなところで生まれたの？ 」

"Nee papa watashi donna tokorode umaretano?"

"Well, Mina, you were born in a city halfway around the world where they speak a different language and eat different kinds of food. You were born in a city called Tokyo. It's bigger than you can imagine – a place that is always bustling."

「ミナが生まれたのは　言葉も食べ物もちがう地球の向こう側　『東京』だよ。

きっと、おまえが思っているよりもずっと大きくてにぎやかなところだよ。」

"Mina ga umareta nowa kotoba mo tabemono mo chigau chikyuu no mukoh-gawa 'Tokyo' dayo. Kitto, omae ga omotte iru yori mo zutto ookikute nigiyakana tokoro dayo."

archer
しゃしゅ
shashu

There are expert archers.

弓道する人を '射手' と呼ぶんだよ。

Kyuudo wo suruhito wo Shashu to yobunodayo.

pagoda
とう
tou

And shrines with pagodas – tall buildings that look like expensive wedding cakes.

お寺の五重の塔はウェデイングケーキみたいだね。

Otera no gojuunotou wa wedding-cake mitai dane.

roasted
chestnuts
あま
ぐり
ama guri

In the winter, there are men on the streets selling hot roasted chestnuts.

寒い冬には甘栗があたたかくておいしいよ。

Samui fuyu niwa amaguri ga atatakakute oishiiyo.

The construction workers wear two-toed shoes and big balloon pants.

大工さんは地下足袋（じかたび）をはいて仕事をするよ。

Daiku-san wa jikatabi wo haite shigoto wo suruyo.

special socks
じかたび
jika tabi

The ravens are big and loud and sometimes snatch food right from your hands!

からすはいつもえさをねらっているから 気をつけて。

Karasu wa itsumo esa wo neratte irukara.
kiwo tsukete.

raven

からす

karasu

daruma
だるま

There are wish dolls called daruma. When you make your wish, you draw one eye. When it comes true, you draw the other.

片方に目を入れて、願いがかなったらもう片方に目を入れるよ。

Kataho ni me wo irete, negai ga kanattara mou katahou ni me wo ireruyo.

ema
えま

Or you can go to the nearby shrine and write your wish on an ema tablet and hang it outside the shrine with all the other wishes.

神社で えま に願いをかきましょう。

Jinja de Ema ni negai wo kakimasho.

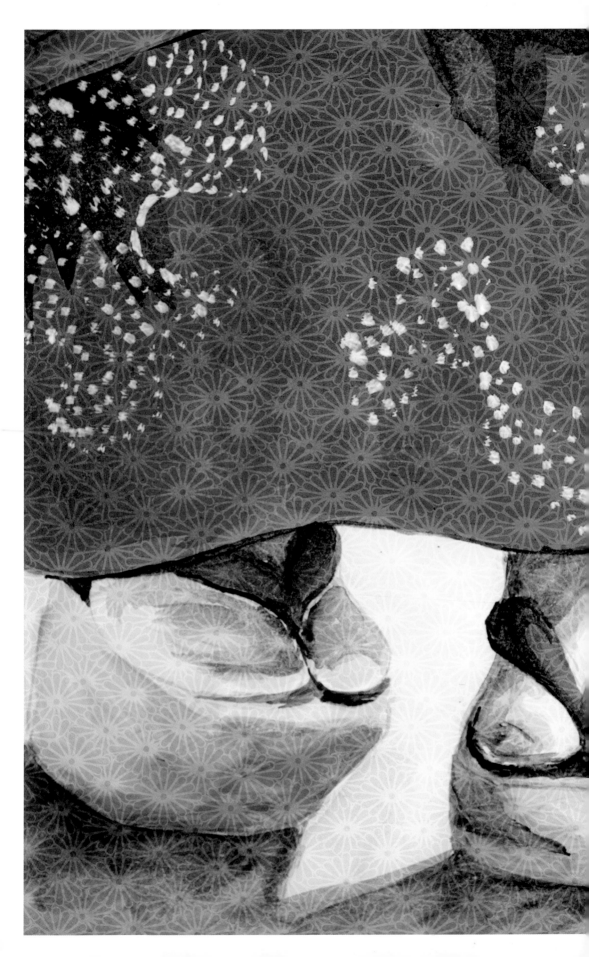

zouri
ぞうり

In the old days, everyone wore shoes called zouri that looked like wooden flip-flops. Some women wore tall zouri to keep their clothes out of the mud.

きものを着たら ぞうりやげたをはくよ。 赤い鼻緒がかわいいね。

Kimono wo ki tara zouri ya geta wo hakuyo. Akai hanao ga kawaii ne.

There are parts of Tokyo where all the boys and girls wear crazy and colorful costumes and you feel like you are in the future.

原宿にはこんな女の子がたくさんいるらしい。　未来都市に迷い込んだみたいだね。

Harajuku niwa konna onnanoko ga takusaniru rashii.
Mirai toshi ni mayoikonda mitai dane.

temple
てら
tera

And other parts where you think you've travelled back in time.

お寺に行ってごらん。昔にタイムスリップしたみたい。

Otera ni itte goran. Mukashi ni time slip shita mitai.

There are kites that look like caterpillars or dragons.

龍の形の凧もあるよ。

Ryu no katachi no tako mo aruyo.

kite

たこ

tako

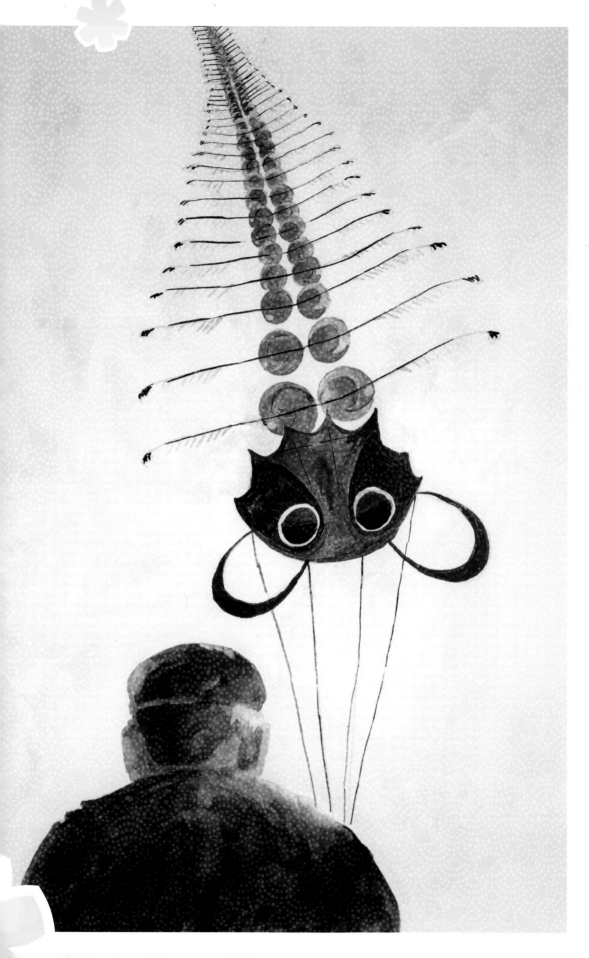

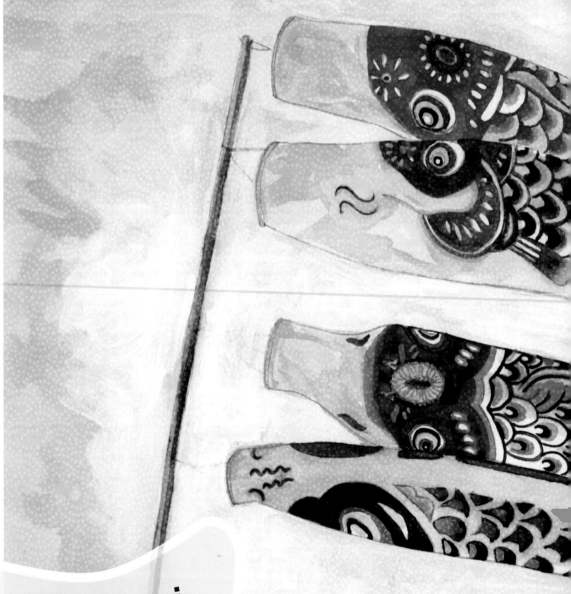

koi-nobori
こいの
ぼり

And there are flags that are especially for children. On Children's Day, the sky is filled with koinobori and it appears as if the sky has turned into the ocean.

こどもの日、空にはこいのぼりが泳ぎます。 元気に育ちますように願いをこめて。

kodomo no hi, sora niwa koi-nobori ga oyogi masu. Genki ni sodachi masu yoni negai wo komete.

koban
こうばん

The police have their own little buildings called koban. There are hundreds of them all over Tokyo.

交番にはおまわりさん、町を守ってくれるよ。

koban niwa omawarisan, machi wo mamotte kureruyo.

Store owners put beckoning kitty dolls, maneki neko, in the window to bring in customers.

お客さんが たくさん来るようにと，店にまねきねこを置くよ。

Okyaku-san ga takusan kuruyounito, mise ni Maneki neko wo okuyo.

maneki neko
まねき
ねこ

In the center of the city, just a few minutes away from the trains and fluorescent lights, you can find one of the most peaceful spots in the world.

にぎやかな東京の中に こんな静かなところがあります。

Nigiyaka na Tokyo no naka ni konna shizukana tokoro ga arimasu.

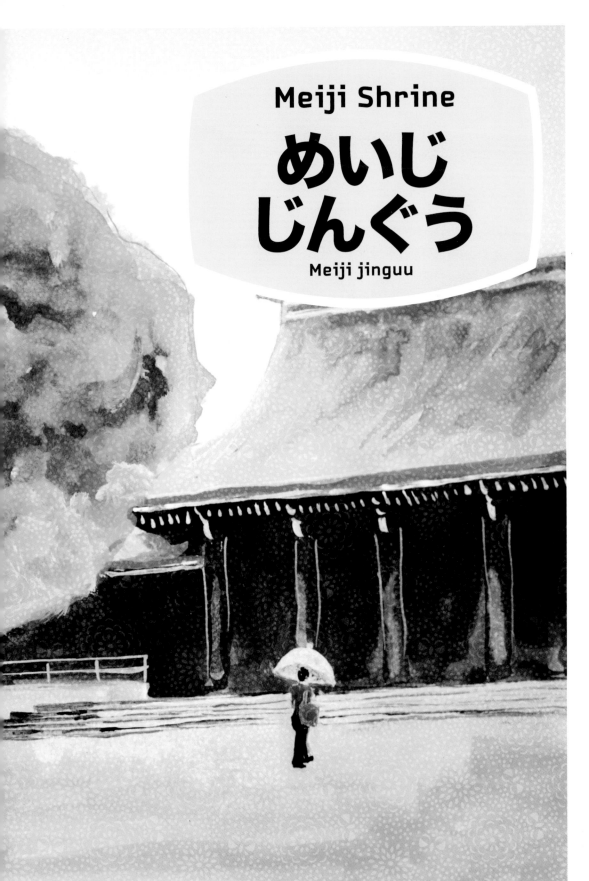

Meiji Shrine

めいじ
じんぐう

Meiji jinguu

Buddhist monk

おぼうさん

obohsan

You might meet a Buddhist monk chanting prayers or meditations.

お経をとなえるおぼうさんにも会えるかな。

Okyou wo tonaeru obohsan nimo aeru kana.

Or you might get a chance to pound rice into omochi.

『おもち』は　もち米を蒸して杵でついてつくります。

Omochi ha mochigome wo mushite kinede tsuite tsukurimasu.

rice cake
おもち
omochi

The public telephones are huge and green.

こうしゅうでんわは大きくてみどりいろ。

koushuu denwa wa ookikute midori iro.

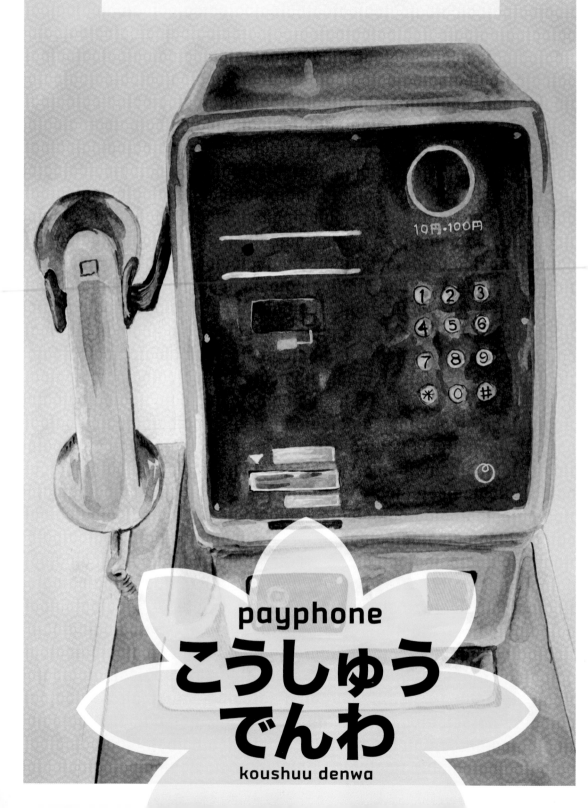

payphone

こうしゅう でんわ

koushuu denwa

mailbox
ぽすと
posuto

The mailboxes are bright red.

ぽすとは赤いよ。

Posuto wa akai yo.

tengu
てんぐ

And the monsters in Tokyo are terrifying!
They have red faces, bulbous noses, and
sharp fangs.

赤い顔にするどい牙。 てんぐは怖いね。

Akai kao ni surudoi kiba. Tengu wa kowai ne.

The ramen noodle shops have bright lanterns outside that say "RAMEN!"

お腹がすいたら、ラーメンやの
ちょうちんを探してみよう。

Onakaga suitara
ramen-ya no chouchin
wo sagashitemiyo.

ramen
らーめん

たこ
やき

Or if you're not in the mood for noodles, you might try fried octopus.

たこやきも食べてみよう。

Takoyaki mo tabete miyou.

300¥

onigiri
おにぎり

You can buy onigiri, little rice balls wrapped in seaweed, at every corner store.

おにぎりは コンビニでも売ってるよ。

Onigiri wa convenience store demo utteiru yo.

The candy has unusual flavors like melon and muscat.

メロン、マスカット、どれが好き？

Meron, mascut, dorega suki？

octopus
たこ
tako

The fish markets have piles of bizarre and fascinating seafood.

市場には魚や蛸や海草がたくさんあるよ。

Ichiba niwa sakana ya tako ya kaisou ga takusan aruyo.

sumo
すもう

Sumo wrestling is one of the oldest sports in Tokyo and the wrestlers can weigh over 500 lbs!

すもうは日本のスポーツ。 おすもうさんはとっても大きくてびっくりするね。

Sumo wa Nippon no sports. Osumoh-san wa totemo ookikute bikkuri surune.

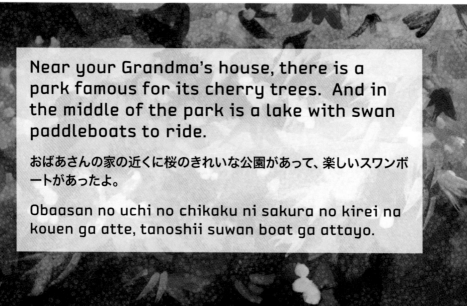

Near your Grandma's house, there is a park famous for its cherry trees. And in the middle of the park is a lake with swan paddleboats to ride.

おばあさんの家の近くに桜のきれいな公園があって、楽しいスワンボートがあったよ。

Obaasan no uchi no chikaku ni sakura no kirei na kouen ga atte, tanoshii suwan boat ga attayo.

paddleboat

あしこぎ ぼーと

ashikogi boat

Japanese drum

たいこ

taiko

And every once in awhile, you'll come across a festival where there is music and dancing and fireworks all night long.

夏まつりはたいこに合わせて盆おどり。
夜空には花火がきれい。

Natsu matsuri wa taiko ni awasete bon-odori. Yozora niwa hanabi ga kirei.

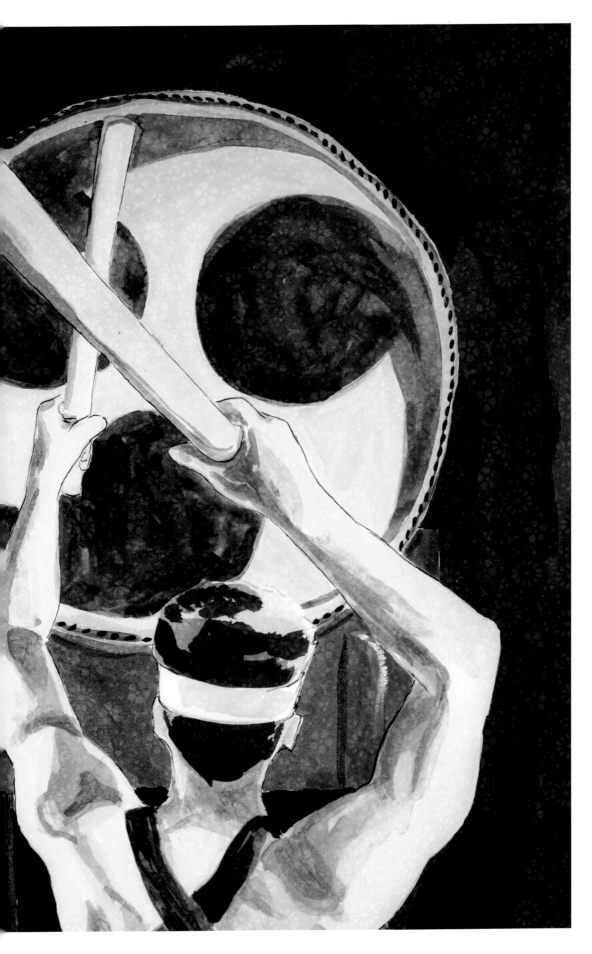

shrine gate
とりい
torii

"Are you making all of this up, papa?"

「東京は本当にこんなに楽しいところなの?」

"Tokyo wa hontouni konnani tanoshii tokoro nano?"

"No, Mina, it's all true. And when you're a little older, we'll go visit Tokyo together. We'll go and eat all the different food, and walk through the parks, and see the temples and shrines, and...

「もちろん。　ミナがもう少し大きくなったらパパと一緒に東京へ行って　お寺や神社を見よう」

"Mochiron. Mina ga mosukoshi ookiku nattara papa to issho ni Tokyo ni itte Otera ya Jinja wo miyou..."

"...track down some ninjas."

「そして　Minaの好きな忍者のことも調べてみよう。」

"Soshite Mina no sukina Ninja no kotomo
shirabete miyou."

MAP OF JAPAN
日本の地図

SEA O

Hirosh

Kitakyushu •
Fukuoka •
Nagasaki •

KYUSHU

Okinawa

JAPAN

HOKKAIDO

Sapporo •

Akita •

• Sendai

HONSHU

とうきょう
★TOKYO

Mt. Fuji ▲
Kyoto •   • Yokohama
        • Nagoya
Kobe • • Osaka

SHIKOKU

NORTH PACIFIC OCEAN

Irene Akio was born in Japan and grew up in Ann Arbor, Michigan with her brother and mother. As a child, she spent many of her summers in Tokyo with her father and the Japanese side of her family. Irene very much considers both Japan and the United States her home, but has been living happily in Seattle, Washington for over five years...as a ninja. Shhh.

アイリーン・アキオ　プロフィール

日本生まれ。
母親の故郷　アメリカ　ミシガン州アナーバーで兄とともに成長する。
夏休みには父親の故郷である日本に何度も訪れ、父方の親戚と過ごしている。

日本とアメリカ、両国への思いが強い彼女だが、現在はワシントン州シアトルで幸せに暮らしている。

まるで「忍者」みたいに・・・